TABLE OF CONTENTS

COUNTRY OVERVIEW: UGANDA AT A GLANCE

History

In the 20th century, Uganda went from being perceived internationally as an Eden incarnate—Britain's "Pearl of Africa"—to being considered the antithesis of Eden, largely because of the extreme actions of post-independence leaders Idi Amin and Milton Obote.

Uganda achieved independence from Great Britain in 1962 without any struggle. The British determined a timetable for withdrawal before local groups had organized an effective nationalist movement. Uganda's political parties emerged in response to impending independence rather than as a means of winning it.

Idi Amin's well-publicized excesses at the expense of Uganda and its citizens were not unique, nor were they the earliest assaults on the nation's rule of law. Amin's predecessor, Milton Obote, suspended the 1962 Constitution and ruled part of Uganda by martial law for five years until a military coup in 1971 brought Amin to power. Obote regained power during the civil war from 1981 to 1985, a period when government troops carried out genocidal sweeps of the rural populace in a region that became known as the Luweero Triangle. The dramatic collapse of the government under Amin, his plunder of the nation's economy, and the even greater failure of the second Obote government in the 1980s certainly had not been expected when the country gained independence. On the contrary, Uganda had been considered a model of stability and potential progress, particularly relative to neighbors Kenya, Tanzania, and Congo.

After years of civil war, Yoweri Kaguta Museveni and the National Resistance Army (NRA) marched on Kampala, and Museveni formally claimed the presidency on January 29, 1986. Museveni's government has been credited with introducing democratic reforms and enhancing human rights. President Museveni was re-elected in 2001 and again in 2006 following a constitutional change that allowed him to run for a third term. Presidential Elections in February 2011 again resulted in a victory for Museveni, with disputes on its validity from opposition parties.

Government

As the NRA gained legitimate control of the government, it became known as the National Resistance Movement (NRM). Until recently, the Ugandan government followed a single or no-party parliamentary system. This system ended in February 2006 with the election of a new parliament, with members representing multiple parties. Despite this change, the NRM continues to control access to political power, as it was the overwhelming winner of these most recent elections.

Although much of Uganda has remained peaceful and stable since Museveni has been in power, some parts of the country are still considered post-conflict areas, particularly in the north and in the west along the border with Congo. Volunteers were assigned to northern areas in 2009 and some areas in the northeast are off-limits for travel.

Economy

Beginning in 1986, Uganda implemented broad economic reforms that can be categorized in two phases. The first phase focused on stabilizing the economy and the second focused on introducing reforms to remove structural distortions in markets. These reforms were successful, and the economy was stabilized by 1992. The International Monetary Fund and the World Bank have repeatedly cited Uganda as an economic success story. Its gross domestic product has averaged a growth rate of 6.3 percent since 1992.

Cash-based agricultural activity still constitutes about 26 percent of GDP and 95 percent of export revenues. In addition, agriculture accounts for more than 90 percent of subsistence economic activity. The government of Uganda has put a lot of emphasis on the improvement of agriculture.

Cash crops include coffee, cotton, tea, tobacco, cut flowers, and vanilla. Food crops include plantains, cassavas, sweet potatoes, millet, sorghum, corn, beans, and groundnuts. Fishing is important for domestic consumption and exportation. Forest covers 7.5 million hectares, but this resource is being rapidly depleted despite attempts at regulation.

The economy has seen a slowdown in recent years, probably because all the easy routes to economic growth have already been taken. Difficult policy and reform decisions lie ahead if the government hopes to continue the economy's uphill climb.

People and Culture

There are three major linguistic families in Uganda and about 50 distinct languages divided among them. Languages also tend to define the boundaries of cultural differences. In the late 1980s, Ugandan officials estimated that 66 percent of the population consisted of Christians (almost equally divided among Protestants and Roman Catholics), approximately 15 percent were Muslim, and roughly 19 percent were adherents of local religions or not affiliated with any religion. World and local religions have coexisted for more than a century in Uganda, and many people have established a coherent set of beliefs about the nature of the universe by combining elements of the two. Except in a few areas, world religions are seldom viewed as incompatible with local religions.

Education is highly valued in much of Uganda. As a result of the government's commitment to universal primary education, primary enrollment jumped from 2.7 million children in 1996 to 6.5 million in 1999. These numbers continue to grow, with nearly 7.4 million students enrolled in 2004. The net primary enrollment rate is estimated at 93 percent, and the gap between boys' and girls' enrollment rates has decreased. For most of the country, the issue is no longer access to primary education, but the quality of that education.

During Uganda's civil wars, the health care system basically collapsed. It is still barely functional outside urban areas, and in certain services, today's care is worse than it was in the 1980s. Life expectancy has increased from 44 to 47 years since 2000. Health, nutrition, and child survival indicators have improved in part because of the government's promotion of immunization to prevent childhood killer diseases such as measles, polio, and whooping cough. However, many infectious diseases remain endemic, including respiratory tract infections, anemia, tetanus, malaria, and tuberculosis.

A significant accomplishment is Uganda's vigorous, effective response to the HIV/AIDS pandemic, with adult HIV infection rates reduced by half over the past 10 years. Nonetheless, about 500,000 Ugandans are living with HIV/AIDS, and 1.7 million children under age 18 have lost one or both parents to AIDS—a number expected to double within the next 10 years. The epidemic has had a tremendous social, economic, and personal impact on the country and its people.

The loss of teachers has crippled education systems, while illness and disability drains family income and forces governments and donors to redirect limited resources from other priorities. The fear and uncertainty AIDS causes has led to increased domestic violence and stigmatizing of people living with HIV/AIDS, isolating them from friends and family and cutting them off from economic opportunities. As a Peace Corps Volunteer, you will confront these issues on a very personal level. It is important to be aware of the high emotional toll that disease, death, and violence can have on Volunteers. As you strive to integrate into your community, you will develop relationships with local people who might die during your service. Because of the AIDS pandemic, some Volunteers will be regularly meeting with HIV-positive people and working with training staff, office staff, and host family members living with AIDS. Volunteers need to prepare themselves to embrace these relationships in a sensitive and positive manner. Likewise, malaria and malnutrition, motor vehicle accidents and other unintentional injuries, domestic violence, and corporal punishment are problems a Volunteer may confront. You will need to anticipate these situations and utilize supportive resources available throughout your training and service to maintain your own emotional strength so you can continue to be of service to your community.

Environment

Uganda's land area is 96,456 square miles, including 17,600 square miles of open water or swampland. Much of the country is a plateau that slopes gently downward toward the north, with a central depression occupied by Lake Kyoga. Mount Elgon and the Rwenzori Mountains form Uganda's borders in the east and west, respectively. Approximately one-half of Lake Victoria, the source of the Nile River, lies within Uganda.

Uganda has an equatorial climate that is moderated by altitude. Average annual rainfall varies from more than 84 inches around Lake Victoria to about 20 inches in the northeast. Vegetation is heaviest in the south, thinning out to savanna and dry plains in the northeast.

RESOURCES FOR FURTHER INFORMATION

Following is a list of websites for additional information about the Peace Corps, Uganda, and to connect you to returned Volunteers and other invitees. Please keep in mind that although we try to make sure all these links are active and current, we cannot guarantee it. If you do not have access to the Internet, visit your local library. Libraries offer free Internet usage and often let you print information to take home.

A note of caution: As you surf the Internet, be aware that you may find bulletin boards and chat rooms in which people are free to express opinions about the Peace Corps based on their own experience, including comments by those who were unhappy with their choice to serve in the Peace Corps. These opinions are not those of the Peace Corps or the U.S. government, and we hope you will keep in mind that no two people experience their service in the same way.

General Information About Uganda

www.countrywatch.com

On this site, you can learn anything from what time it is in the capital of Uganda to how to convert from the dollar to the Uganda currency. Just click on Uganda and go from there.

www.lonelyplanet.com/destinations

Visit this site for general travel advice about almost any country in the world.

www.state.gov

The State Department's website issues background notes periodically about countries around the world. Find Uganda and learn more about its social and political history. You can also go to the site's international travel section to check on conditions that may affect your safety.

www.psr.keele.ac.uk/official.htm

This includes links to all the official sites for governments worldwide.

www.geography.about.com/library/maps/blindex.htm

This online world atlas includes maps and geographical information, and each country page contains links to other sites, such as the Library of Congress, that contain comprehensive historical, social, and political background.

www.cyberschoolbus.un.org/infonation/info.asp

This United Nations site allows you to search for statistical information for member states of the U.N.

www.worldinformation.com

This site provides an additional source of current and historical information about countries around the world.

Connect With Returned Volunteers and Other Invitees

www.rpcv.org

This is the site of the National Peace Corps Association, made up of returned Volunteers. On this site you can find links to all the Web pages of the "Friends of" groups for most countries of service, comprised of former Volunteers who served in those countries. There are also regional groups that frequently get together for social events and local volunteer activities. Or go straight to the Friends of Uganda site: **www.friendsofuganda.org.**

www.PeaceCorpsWorldwide.org

This site is hosted by a group of returned Volunteer writers. It is a monthly online publication of essays and Volunteer accounts of their Peace Corps service.

Online Articles/Current News Sites About Uganda

www.buganda.com

This site offers a wealth of information about the central Buganda area of Uganda.

www.unaids.org

This United Nations site includes thorough information about the AIDS pandemic.

http://www.bbc.co.uk/news/world/africa/

This BBC site features headlines about Africa (search for Uganda).

http://allafrica.com

Access this site to search for news about Uganda.

www.csmonitor.com

This Christian Science Monitor site allows you to search for stories on Uganda.

International Development Sites About Uganda

www.worldbank.org/afr/ug/

This features information on the World Bank's projects in Uganda.

www.africaaction.org/index.php

Site of the U.S.-based organization Africa Action, which works for political, economic, and social justice in Africa.

www.bellanet.org/

Bellanet helps the international community collaborate more effectively, especially by use of information technology.

Recommended Books

- Baingana, Doreen. *Tropical Fish: Tales from Entebbe*. Harlem Moon, New York, 2005.

- Eichstaedt, Peter. *First Kill Your Family: Child Soldiers of Uganda and the Lord's Resistance Army*. 2009.

- Isegawa, Moses. *Abyssinian Chronicles*. New York: Knopf, 2000.

- McDonnell, Faith and Grace Akallo. *Girl Soldier: A Story of Hope for Northern Uganda's Children*. 2009.

- Museveni, Yoweni Kaguta. *Sowing the Mustard Seed: The Struggle for Freedom and Democracy in Uganda*. London: Macmillan Education, 1997.

- Rice, Andrew. *The Teeth May Smile but the Heart Does Not Forget*, New York: Metropolitan Books, 2009

- Twaddle, Michael, and Holger B. Hansen (eds.). *Uganda Now: Between Decay and Development*. London: James Curry, 1989.

- Twaddle, Michael, and Holger B. Hansen (eds.). *Changing Uganda: The Dilemmas of Structural Adjustment and Revolutionary Change*. London: James Curry, 1991.

- Wallman, Sandra. *Kampala Women Getting by: Wellbeing in the Time of AIDS*. London: James Currey, 1996.

Books About the History of the Peace Corps

- Hoffman, Elizabeth Cobbs. *All You Need is Love: The Peace Corps and the Spirit of the 1960s*. Cambridge, Mass.: Harvard University Press, 2000.

- Rice, Gerald T. *The Bold Experiment: JFK's Peace Corps*. Notre Dame, Ind.: University of Notre Dame Press, 1985.

- Stossel, Scott. *Sarge: The Life and Times of Sargent Shriver*. Washington, D.C.: Smithsonian Institution Press, 2004.

- Meisler, Stanley. *When the World Calls: The Inside Story of the Peace Corps and its First 50 Years*. Boston, Mass.: Beacon Press, 2011.

Books on the Volunteer Experience

- Dirlam, Sharon. *Beyond Siberia: Two Years in a Forgotten Place*. Santa Barbara, Calif.: McSeas Books, 2004.

- Casebolt, Marjorie DeMoss. *Margarita: A Guatemalan Peace Corps Experience*. Gig Harbor, Wash.: Red Apple Publishing, 2000.

- Erdman, Sarah. Nine Hills to Nambonkaha: Two Years in the Heart of an African Village. New York, N.Y.: Picador, 2003.

- Hessler, Peter. *River Town: Two Years on the Yangtze*. New York, N.Y.: Perennial, 2001.

- Kennedy, Geraldine ed. *From the Center of the Earth: Stories out of the Peace Corps*. Santa Monica, Calif.: Clover Park Press, 1991.

- Thompsen, Moritz. *Living Poor: A Peace Corps Chronicle*. Seattle, Wash.: University of Washington Press, 1997 (reprint).

LIVING CONDITIONS AND VOLUNTEER LIFESTYLE

Communications
Mail

Few countries in the world offer the level of service considered normal in the United States. If you expect U.S. standards for mail service, you will be in for some frustration. Letters take a minimum of two weeks to arrive in Uganda if sent by airmail; packages even longer. Packages sent by surface mail usually take between one and two months. Some mail may simply not arrive (this is not a frequent occurrence, but it does happen). Advise your friends and family to number their letters for tracking purposes and to write "Airmail" and "Par Avion" on their envelopes. If someone sends you a package, it is best to keep it small and use a padded envelope so it will be treated as a letter. Valuables should not be sent through the mail.

Despite the delays, we encourage you to write to your family regularly and to number your letters. Family members typically become worried when they do not hear from you, so it is a good idea to advise them that mail service is sporadic and that they should not be concerned if they do not receive letters from you regularly. This is especially true at the beginning, when you will be involved in an intense training program.

Your address during training will be:

"Your Name," PCT
P.O. Box 29348
Kampala, Uganda

After training, you will be expected to establish a mailing address in the community where you are posted. Let family know that the address listed above will be a temporary one used during your first few months in Uganda.

Telephones

You will have limited access to email during training.

Almost every Uganda Peace Corps Volunteer has a cell phone. Network coverage varies depending on where you are assigned, but networks are continuously expanding. Some Volunteers have difficulty charging their phones, but Volunteers always find a way to communicate with family, fellow Volunteers, and Peace Corps staff. Incoming calls on cell phones are free, but outgoing calls, especially those to America, are very expensive. Advise your family and friends in America to use phone cards.

Computer, Internet, and Email Access

A Volunteer advises the following: Regardless of the field you are working in, the majority of Volunteers are grateful for the addition of a small laptop computer during their service. For project organization, informal technology education or escaping into your favorite American sitcom, a computer is invaluable.

Considerations:

- Netbook computers are lighter and more packable and compete with computers in terms of speed and battery life. Furthermore, their small power output allows for the possibility of solar charging for those villages fully off the grid. Get a 6-cell battery instead of 3 cell. You'll appreciate those extra hours between charges.

- There is an enormous body of media available in the Peace Corps Volunteer Lounge—enough to fill any computer hard drive several times over. Most Volunteers have external drives (500 gig minimum) to aid in program, video, and teaching and development materials exchange. This allows you to travel lighter when all you want is to grab a digital book from your nearest Volunteer.

- Believe it or not, you can connect to the Internet through your cellphone provider almost anywhere in Uganda. USB modems are available for less than USD 35.00 and service charges are fully affordable.

Most of us moved to Africa with the idea that we'd be on a two-year backpacking trip. What we found was a country connected top to bottom with technology for those who can afford it! Embracing this technology has made us better Volunteers. The use of computers allows us to stay in better touch with each other in the field and with our families in the U.S. We can build capacity by introducing technology to the forces that are flattening our world, specifically the free exchange of ideas and information.

Please remember when deciding whether or not to bring a laptop, Peace Corps is in no way liable for a lost, stolen or damaged computer. It's advisable to get property insurance for laptops and any other personal items of value.

Access to email and the Internet is available at Internet cafes in most major towns in Uganda. Most Volunteers check email weekly, depending on personal choice and site location. While Internet is slow at times, you will be able to communicate through email and/or blogs.

Housing and Site Location

During your service, you will most likely live in a rural area in very modest accommodations provided by your host organization, which will try to provide you with at least a bedroom and a sitting room. You might live in part of a Ugandan family's house or in part of a house built for staff of a school or community organization. It is unlikely that you will share your accommodations with anyone else unless you choose to do so.

Living conditions vary according to the resources of the community or organization in which you are placed. Most houses do not have running water or electricity. You should expect to use a pit latrine and a kerosene lantern and stove. Most Volunteers hire someone to carry water to their house. The community may provide some basic furnishings, and you can supplement these with your modest settling-in allowance provided by the Peace Corps. At nearly all sites, the kind of privacy that most Americans are used to will be extremely limited. Children may be around constantly, demonstrating their curiosity about you. You will have to adapt to a more public life.

As most communities and organizations have extremely limited resources, providing housing and furnishing is a great sacrifice. Sometimes there are delays in obtaining housing or furnishings. You might have to stay in temporary accommodations while your permanent housing is being set up.

Although the Peace Corps staff makes every effort to collaborate with communities to see that housing is ready for Volunteers when they arrive at their sites, you should be prepared to gratefully accept whatever the community provides, no matter how basic.

Living Allowance and Money Management

As a Volunteer, you will receive a modest living allowance, paid in local currency that will allow you to live on par with your colleagues and co-workers. The amount of this allowance is based on regular surveys of Volunteers and the cost of living in Uganda. The allowance is paid quarterly into bank accounts set up for Volunteers, so the ability to manage funds wisely is important. The current living allowance is equivalent to approximately $250 per month and is meant to cover the cost of food, utilities, household supplies, clothing, recreation and entertainment, reading materials, and other incidentals. You may find that you receive more remuneration than your counterpart or supervisor.

You will also receive a leave allowance of $24 per month (standard in all Peace Corps countries), which is paid in local currency along with your living allowance.

Current Volunteers suggest that you bring cash and credit cards if you plan to travel during vacations. Very few establishments in Uganda accept credit cards, so they are mainly useful for travel to other countries. The amount of cash you will need depends on the amount of traveling you plan to do while serving in Uganda (Volunteers earn two days of leave per month of service, excluding training). Peace Corps will set up a bank account for you. Banks can be found in all major cities/towns and you will be able to access funds. Peace Corps deposits your monthly living allowance at the beginning of each month and you are responsible for withdrawing the amount you need. The exchange rate is approximately 2200 Ugandan shillings to the U.S. dollar, but the exchange rate changes frequently.

Food and Diet

You will buy your food from outdoor markets or small shops, and you will generally cook for yourself. The local diet is basic but healthy, including a variety of fruits, vegetables, starches, and meats. There are likely to be some local food restaurants at or near your site. Imported foods, while expensive, can be found in larger towns and serve as a great treat. During training, there will be sessions on safe food preparation and proper nutrition. It is relatively easy to follow a vegetarian diet in Uganda after one becomes familiar with the local food. Most Ugandans will not be prepared to serve a vegetarian meal if you are a guest in their home, but will generally accept a sensitive explanation of your dietary preferences.

Transportation

Volunteers travel primarily by foot, bicycle, or public transport. Public transportation to and from the nearest urban or trading center is available near every site; in most cases several times a day. Public transport is likely to be crowded, uncomfortable, and unreliable! To facilitate fieldwork, Volunteers are given an allowance to purchase a bike. Still, many of the communities and jobsites Volunteers visit may entail a long and challenging ride. Some Volunteers must be able to ride a bicycle in order to do their jobs. Please come to Uganda with this as an expectation.

The Peace Corps/Uganda prohibits the use of motorcycles by Volunteers because of the extreme safety risks they pose. When using a bicycle, Volunteers must wear helmets (provided by Peace Corps).

Geography and Climate

Uganda straddles the equator, which means that the seasons are quite different from those in the United States. Rather than a hot season and a cold one, there are rainy seasons and dry seasons. Rainy periods generally occur in November and December and in April and May. The climate around Lake Victoria is greatly influenced by the lake. As a result, rain can occur there at any time. Midday temperatures are in the 70s and 80s (depending upon the part of the country) in all seasons, but evenings are cooler and may require wearing a sweater or light jacket.

Social Activities

The most common form of entertainment is socializing among friends and neighbors. Some Volunteers visit other Volunteers on weekends or holidays. The Peace Corps encourages Volunteers to remain at their sites as much as possible to develop relationships with community members, but it also recognizes the need to make infrequent trips to regional centers and to visit friends.

Uganda has several rural radio stations, and many Volunteers bring radios so they can listen to international broadcasts by the BBC, Voice of America, and Deutsche Welle. Some larger towns have cinemas as well.

You will find it easy to make friends in your community and to participate in weddings, funerals, birthday celebrations, and other social events. It is impossible to overemphasize the rewards of establishing rapport with one's supervisors, co-workers, and other community members. A sincere effort to learn the local language will greatly facilitate these interactions.

Professionalism, Dress, and Behavior

Norms for dress are much more conservative in Uganda than in the United States, where some view our clothes as an expression of our individuality. Ugandans view dressing appropriately as a sign of respect for others. Wearing clothes that are dirty, have holes in them, or are too revealing sends the message that the people you are interacting with are not worth greater care. Dressing in neat, clean, and conservative clothes, on the other hand, can ease your integration into your new community and enhance your professional credibility and effectiveness.

Many Ugandan men wear slacks, button-up shirts, and ties in professional settings. Blue jeans, T-shirts, and casual sandals are not considered appropriate in the workplace, during training, or during visits to the Peace Corps office. Women wear skirts that reach the middle of the knee or below with tops in both professional and nonprofessional environments; short skirts and low-cut or sleeveless tops are highly inappropriate, particularly in rural settings. Male Volunteers must wear their hair short and neat. Volunteers doing fieldwork generally should wash and change their clothes before returning to a public area. When riding bicycles, women wear skirts, capris, or gouchos.

Facial piercing should be kept to a minimum, with discreet studs—avoid hoops for security and for cultural reasons. If you have tattoos, it will be expected that you keep them covered, especially when you are in your community.

If you have reservations about your ability to adapt to Ugandan norms of dress and appearance, you should re-evaluate your decision to become a Volunteer. Working effectively in another culture requires a certain level of sacrifice and flexibility, and the Peace Corps expects Volunteers to behave in a manner that will foster respect within their communities and reflect well upon the Peace Corps. Behavior that jeopardizes your safety or the presence of the Peace Corps program in Uganda could lead to administrative separation—a decision by the Peace Corps to terminate your service.

Personal Safety

More detailed information about the Peace Corps' approach to safety is contained in the "Health Care and Safety" chapter, but it is an important issue and cannot be overemphasized. As stated in the Volunteer Handbook, becoming a Peace Corps Volunteer entails certain safety risks. Living and traveling in an unfamiliar environment (oftentimes alone), having a limited understanding of local language and culture, and being perceived as well-off are some of the factors that can put a Volunteer at risk. Many Volunteers experience varying degrees of unwanted attention and harassment. Petty thefts and burglaries are not uncommon, and incidents of physical and sexual assault do occur, although most Uganda Volunteers complete their two years of service without incident. The Peace Corps has established procedures and policies designed to help you reduce your risks and enhance your safety and security. These procedures and policies, in addition to safety training, will be provided once you arrive in Uganda. Using these tools, you are expected to take responsibility for your safety and well-being.

Each staff member at the Peace Corps is committed to providing Volunteers with the support they need to successfully meet the challenges they will face to have a safe, healthy, and productive service. We encourage Volunteers and families to look at our safety and security information on the Peace Corps website at **www.peacecorps.gov/safety**.

Information on these pages gives messages on Volunteer health and Volunteer safety. There is a section titled "Safety and Security – Our Partnership." Among topics addressed are the risks of serving as a Volunteer, posts' safety support systems, and emergency planning and communications.

Rewards and Frustrations

Although the potential for job satisfaction in Uganda is quite high, like all Volunteers, you will encounter frustrations. Perceptions of time are very different from those in America. The lack of basic infrastructure can become very tiring, and social demands on your colleagues may mean their work habits vary greatly from yours. For these reasons, the Peace Corps experience of adapting to a new culture and environment is often described as a series of emotional peaks and valleys.

You will be given a great deal of responsibility and independence in your work—perhaps more than in any other job you have had or will have. You will often need to motivate yourself and others with little guidance from supervisors. You might work for months without seeing any visible impact from, or without receiving feedback on, your work. Development is a slow process. You must possess the self-confidence, patience, and vision—tempered with humility and the resulting respect for others—to continue working toward long-term goals without seeing immediate results.

To overcome these difficulties, you will also need maturity, flexibility, open-mindedness, resourcefulness, and, most importantly, a sense of humor. Most Volunteers manage to exhibit enough of these characteristics to serve successfully. Judging by the experience of former Volunteers, the peaks are well worth the difficult times, and most Volunteers leave Uganda feeling they have gained much more than they sacrificed during their service. If you are able to make the commitment to integrate into your community and to focus on the community's interests, your service is likely to be a life-altering experience.

PEACE CORPS TRAINING

Pre-Service Training

Pre-service training will provide you with the knowledge and skills you need to integrate into your community and begin to work with your Ugandan counterparts in formal and informal settings. Training provides a friendly and safe environment in which to ask questions and learn about life in Uganda. The 10-week program covers a variety of topics, including language, cross-cultural communication, area studies, development issues, health and personal safety, and technical skills pertinent to your specific assignment.

The pre-service training in Uganda is community-based, which means most of the training sessions take place in a community as similar as possible to actual Volunteer sites. After your arrival in Uganda, you will spend a few days at a central training facility to recover from jet lag and learn a few basics. You might live with a Ugandan host family for all or part of the training in the community chosen to host training. This gives you the opportunity to observe and participate in Ugandan culture and to practice your language skills.

At the onset of training, staff will outline the goals of training and the criteria that will be used to assess your progress. Evaluation during training is a continual process, characterized by a dialogue between you and the training staff, which is ready to work with you toward the highest possible achievement of training goals. Upon successful completion of pre-service training, you will be sworn in as a Volunteer and depart for your site.

Technical Training

Technical training will prepare you to work in Uganda by building on the skills you already have and helping you develop new skills in a manner appropriate to the needs of the country. The Peace Corps staff, Uganda experts, and current Volunteers will conduct the training program. Training places great emphasis on learning how to transfer the skills you have to the community in which you will serve as a Volunteer.

Technical training will include sessions on the general economic and political environment in Uganda and strategies for working within such a framework. You will review your technical sector's goals and will meet with the Uganda agencies and organizations that invited the Peace Corps to assist them. You will be supported and evaluated throughout the training to build the confidence and skills you need to undertake your project activities and be a productive member of your community.

Language Training

As a Peace Corps Volunteer, you will find that language skills are key to personal and professional satisfaction during your service. These skills are critical to your job performance, they help you integrate into your community, and they can ease your personal adaptation to the new surroundings. Therefore, language training is at the heart of the training program. You must successfully meet minimum language requirements to complete training and become a Volunteer. Uganda language instructors teach formal language classes five days a week in small groups of four to five people.

Your language training will incorporate a community-based approach. In addition to classroom time, you will be given assignments to work on outside of the classroom and with your host family. The goal is to get you to a point of basic social communication skills so you can practice and develop language skills further once you are at your site. Prior to being sworn in as a Volunteer, you will work on strategies to continue language studies during your service.

Cross-Cultural Training

As part of your pre-service training, you will live with a Uganda host family. This experience is designed to ease your transition to life at your site. Families go through an orientation conducted by Peace Corps staff to explain the purpose of pre-service training and to assist them in helping you adapt to living in Uganda. Many Volunteers form strong and lasting friendships with their host families.

Cross-cultural and community development training will help you improve your communication skills and understand your role as a facilitator of development. You will be exposed to topics such as community mobilization, conflict resolution, gender and development, nonformal and adult education strategies, and political structures.

Health Training

During pre-service training, you will be given basic medical training and information. You will be expected to practice preventive health care and to take responsibility for your own health by adhering to all medical policies. Trainees are required to attend all medical sessions. The topics include preventive health measures and minor and major medical issues that you might encounter while in Uganda. Nutrition, mental health, setting up a safe living compound, and how to avoid HIV/AIDS and other sexually transmitted diseases (STDs) are also covered.

Safety Training

During the safety training sessions, you will learn how to adopt a lifestyle that reduces your risks at home, at work, and during your travels. You will also learn appropriate, effective strategies for coping with unwanted attention and about your individual responsibility for promoting safety throughout your service.

Additional Trainings During Volunteer Service

In its commitment to institutionalize quality training, the Peace Corps has implemented a training system that provides Volunteers with continual opportunities to examine their commitment to Peace Corps service while increasing their technical and cross-cultural skills. During service, there are usually three training events. The titles and objectives for those trainings are as follows:

- In-service training: Provides an opportunity for Volunteers to upgrade their technical, language, and project development skills while sharing their experiences and reaffirming their commitment after having served for three to six months.

- Midterm conference (done in conjunction with technical sector in-service): Assists Volunteers in reviewing their first year, reassessing their personal and project objectives, and planning for their second year of service.

- Close-of-service conference: Prepares Volunteers for the future after Peace Corps service and reviews their respective projects and personal experiences.

The number, length, and design of these trainings are adapted to country-specific needs and conditions. The key to the training system is that training events are integrated and interrelated, from the pre-departure orientation through the end of your service, and are planned, implemented, and evaluated cooperatively by the training staff, Peace Corps staff, and Volunteers.

YOUR HEALTH CARE AND SAFETY IN UGANDA

The Peace Corps' highest priority is maintaining the good health and safety of every Volunteer. Peace Corps medical programs emphasize the preventive, rather than the curative, approach to disease. The Peace Corps in Uganda maintains a clinic with a full-time medical officer, who takes care of Volunteers' primary health care needs. Additional medical services, such as testing and basic treatment, are also available in Uganda at local hospitals. If you become seriously ill, you will be transported either to an American-standard medical facility in the region or to the United States.

Health Issues in Uganda

Major health problems among Volunteers in Uganda are rare and are often the result of Volunteers not taking preventive measures to stay healthy. The most common health problems in Uganda are relatively minor ones that are also found in the United States, such as colds, diarrhea, skin infections, headaches, dental problems, adjustment disorders, and alcohol abuse. These problems may be more frequent or compounded by life in Uganda because certain environmental factors raise the risk or exacerbate the severity of illnesses and injuries.

The most serious health concerns are malaria, HIV/AIDS, and traffic accidents. Because malaria is endemic in Uganda, taking antimalarial pills is mandated by the Peace Corps. Diarrheal diseases are also common, but can be avoided by regularly washing your hands, thoroughly washing fruits and vegetables, and either boiling your drinking water or using the water purification tablets issued in your medical kit. You will be vaccinated against hepatitis A and B, meningitis A and C, tetanus, diphtheria, typhoid, and rabies.

Helping You Stay Healthy

The Peace Corps will provide you with all the necessary inoculations, medications, and information to stay healthy. Upon your arrival in Uganda, you will receive a medical handbook. At the end of training, you will receive a medical kit with supplies to take care of mild illnesses and first aid needs. The contents of the kit are listed later in this chapter.

During pre-service training, you will have access to basic medical supplies through the medical officer. However, you will be responsible for your own supply of prescription drugs and any other specific medical supplies you require, as the Peace Corps will not order these items during training. Please bring a three-month supply of any prescription drugs you use, since they may not be available here and it may take several months for shipments to arrive.

You will have physicals at midservice and at the end of your service. If you develop a serious medical problem during your service, the medical officer in Uganda will consult with the Office of Medical Services in Washington, D.C. If it is determined that your condition cannot be treated in Uganda, you may be sent out of the country for further evaluation and care.

Maintaining Your Health

As a Volunteer, you must accept considerable responsibility for your own health. Proper precautions will significantly reduce your risk of serious illness or injury. The adage "An ounce of prevention ..." becomes extremely important in areas where diagnostic and treatment facilities are not up to the standards of the United States. The most important of your responsibilities in Uganda is to take the following preventive measures:

Malaria is a major health issue in Uganda. The most important step in preventing malaria and many other tropical diseases is to avoid being bitten by mosquitoes and other insects. The best way to avoid insect bites is to sleep under a treated mosquito net provided by Peace Corps, wear long sleeves and long trousers whenever possible (especially when outside at night), use insect repellent, and make sure windows have some kind of screen. Since no one can entirely prevent insect bites, you must also take antimalarial pills.

Rabies is prevalent throughout Uganda, so you will receive a series of immunizations against it after you arrive. If you are exposed to an animal that is known to have, or suspected of having, rabies, inform the medical officer at once so you can receive post-exposure booster shots. Be wary of all unknown animals and of behavior changes in known animals.

Many illnesses that afflict Volunteers worldwide are entirely preventable if proper food and water precautions are taken. These illnesses include food poisoning, parasitic infections, hepatitis A, dysentery, Guinea worms, tapeworms, and typhoid fever. Your medical officer will discuss specific standards for water and food preparation in Uganda during pre-service training.

Abstinence is the only certain choice for preventing infection with HIV and other sexually transmitted diseases. You are taking risks if you choose to be sexually active. To lessen risk, use a condom every time you have sex. Whether your partner is a host country citizen, a fellow Volunteer, or anyone else, do not assume this person is free of HIV/AIDS or other STDs. You will receive more information from the medical officer about this important issue.

Volunteers are expected to adhere to an effective means of birth control to prevent an unplanned pregnancy. Your medical officer can help you decide on the most appropriate method to suit your individual needs. Contraceptive methods are available without charge from the medical officer.

It is critical to your health that you promptly report to the medical office or other designated facility for scheduled immunizations, and that you let the medical officer know immediately of significant illnesses and injuries.

Women's Health Information

Pregnancy is treated in the same manner as other Volunteer health conditions that require medical attention but also have programmatic ramifications. The Peace Corps is responsible for determining the medical risk and the availability of appropriate medical care if the Volunteer remains in-country. Given the circumstances under which Volunteers live and work in Peace Corps countries, it is rare that the Peace Corps' medical and programmatic standards for continued service during pregnancy can be met.

If feminine hygiene products are not available for you to purchase on the local market, the Peace Corps medical officer in Uganda will provide them. If you require a specific product, please bring a three-month supply with you.

Your Peace Corps Medical Kit

The Peace Corps medical officer will provide you with a kit that contains basic items necessary to prevent and treat illnesses that may occur during service. Kit items can be periodically restocked at the medical office.

Medical Kit Contents

Ace bandages
Adhesive tape
American Red Cross First Aid & Safety Handbook
Antacid tablets (Tums)
Antibiotic ointment (Bacitracin/Neomycin/Polymycin B)
Antiseptic antimicrobial skin cleaner (Hibiclens)
Band-Aids
Butterfly closures
Calamine lotion
Cepacol lozenges
Condoms

Dental floss
Diphenhydramine HCL 25 mg (Benadryl)
Insect repellent stick (Cutter's)
Iodine tablets (for water purification)
Lip balm (Chapstick)
Oral rehydration salts
Oral thermometer (Fahrenheit)
Pseudoephedrine HCL 30 mg (Sudafed)
Robitussin-DM lozenges (for cough)
Scissors
Sterile gauze pads
Tetrahydrozaline eyedrops (Visine)
Tinactin (antifungal cream)
Tweezers

Before You Leave: A Medical Checklist

If there has been any change in your health – physical, mental, or dental – since you submitted your examination reports to the Peace Corps, you must immediately notify the Office of Medical Services. Failure to disclose new illnesses, injuries, allergies, or pregnancy can endanger your health and may jeopardize your eligibility to serve.

If your dental exam was done more than a year ago, or if your physical exam is more than two years old, contact the Office of Medical Services to find out whether you need to update your records. If your dentist or Peace Corps dental consultant has recommended that you undergo dental treatment or repair, you must complete that work and make sure your dentist sends requested confirmation reports or X-rays to the Office of Medical Services.

If you wish to avoid having duplicate vaccinations, contact your physician's office to obtain a copy of your immunization record and bring it to your pre-departure orientation. If you have any immunizations prior to Peace Corps service, the Peace Corps cannot reimburse you for the cost. The Peace Corps will provide all the immunizations necessary for your overseas assignment, either at your pre-departure orientation or shortly after you arrive in Uganda. You do not need to begin taking malaria medication prior to departure.

Bring a three-month supply of any prescription or over-the-counter medication you use on a regular basis, including birth control pills. Although the Peace Corps cannot reimburse you for this three-month supply, it will order refills during your service. While awaiting shipment – which can take several months – you will be dependent on your own medication supply. The Peace Corps will not pay for herbal or nonprescribed medications, such as St. John's wort, glucosamine, selenium, or antioxidant supplements.

You are encouraged to bring copies of medical prescriptions signed by your physician. This is not a requirement, but they might come in handy if you are questioned in transit about carrying a three-month supply of prescription drugs.

If you wear eyeglasses, bring two pairs with you – a pair and a spare. If a pair breaks, the Peace Corps will replace them, using the information your doctor in the United States provided on the eyeglasses form during your examination. The Peace Corps discourages you from using contact lenses during your service to reduce your risk of developing a serious infection or other eye disease. Most Peace Corps countries do not have appropriate water and sanitation to support eye care with the use of contact lenses. The Peace Corps will not supply or replace contact lenses or associated solutions unless an ophthalmologist has recommended their use for a specific medical condition and the Peace Corps' Office of Medical Services has given approval.

If you are eligible for Medicare, are over 50 years of age, or have a health condition that may restrict your future participation in health care plans, you may wish to consult an insurance specialist about unique coverage needs before your departure. The Peace Corps will provide all necessary health care from the time you leave for your pre-departure orientation until you complete your service. When you finish, you will be entitled to the post-service health care benefits described in the Peace Corps Volunteer Handbook. You may wish to consider keeping an existing health plan in effect during your service if you think age or pre-existing conditions might prevent you from re-enrolling in your current plan when you return home.

SAFETY AND SECURITY:
OUR PARTNERSHIP

Serving as a Volunteer overseas entails certain safety and security risks. Living and traveling in an unfamiliar environment, a limited understanding of the local language and culture, and the perception of being a wealthy American are some of the factors that can put a Volunteer at risk. Property theft and burglaries are not uncommon. Incidents of physical and sexual assault do occur, although almost all Volunteers complete their two years of service without serious personal safety problems.

Beyond knowing that Peace Corps approaches safety and security as a partnership with you, it might be helpful to see how this partnership works. Peace Corps has policies, procedures, and training in place to promote your safety. We depend on you to follow those policies and to put into practice what you have learned. An example of how this works in practice – in this case to help manage the risk of burglary – is:

- Peace Corps assesses the security environment where you will live and work
- Peace Corps inspects the house where you will live according to established security criteria
- Peace Corps provides you with resources to take measures such as installing new locks
- Peace Corps ensures you are welcomed by host country authorities in your new community
- Peace Corps responds to security concerns that you raise
- You lock your doors and windows
- You adopt a lifestyle appropriate to the community where you live
- You get to know neighbors
- You decide if purchasing personal articles insurance is appropriate for you
- You don't change residences before being authorized by Peace Corps
- You communicate concerns that you have to Peace Corps staff

Factors that Contribute to Volunteer Risk

There are several factors that can heighten a Volunteer's risk, many of which are within the Volunteer's control. By far the most common crime that Volunteers experience is theft. Thefts often occur when Volunteers are away from their sites, in crowded locations (such as markets or on public transportation), and when leaving items unattended.

Before you depart for Uganda there are several measures you can take to reduce your risk:

- Leave valuable objects in the U.S.

- Leave copies of important documents and account numbers with someone you trust in the U.S.

- Purchase a hidden money pouch or "dummy" wallet as a decoy

- Purchase personal articles insurance

After you arrive in Uganda, you will receive more detailed information about common crimes, factors that contribute to Volunteer risk, and local strategies to reduce that risk. For example, Volunteers in Uganda learn to:

- Choose safe routes and times for travel, and travel with someone trusted by the community whenever possible

- Make sure one's personal appearance is respectful of local customs

- Avoid high-crime areas

- Know the local language to get help in an emergency

- Make friends with local people who are respected in the community

- Limit alcohol consumption

As you can see from this list, you must be willing to work hard and adapt your lifestyle to minimize the potential for being a target for crime. As with anywhere in the world, crime does exist in Uganda. You can reduce your risk by avoiding situations that place you at risk and by taking precautions. Crime at the village or town level is less frequent than in the large cities; people know each other and generally are less likely to steal from their neighbors. Tourist attractions in large towns are favorite worksites for pickpockets.

The following are other security concerns in Uganda of which you should be aware:

While you may be much more likely to be pick-pocketed in crowded areas of Kampala, there is a "borrowing" culture in rural areas, which may cause your property to disappear. Ugandans do not have the same concept of private property as Americans, and if you leave something where it could be taken, even within your compound or house, a local may take it without asking if they perceive that you are either not currently using it or you own too much. Traditionally, when "borrowing" things that are not currently in use, the borrower must eventually return the items to the owner, but when it comes to foreigners, items are seldom returned.

Years ago Kampala was the site of infrequent rebel activities, which are otherwise restricted to the far north or west. They took the form of small-scale attacks in busy, populated areas. Although no Volunteers were harmed in these attacks, the potential for harm exists, and the Peace Corps program in Uganda was suspended in 1999 as a result of such attacks. With the program's reopening in 2001, several program changes were made to enhance Volunteer safety and the sustainability of the program as a whole. One of these changes is that Volunteers placed outside of Kampala may not travel to Kampala without an official reason and without prior approval from their program manager or Peace Corps medical officer. In late 2007, Uganda was considered free from rebel activities and Peace Corps has Volunteer placements in the North and Northwestern region, however the Karamoja (Northeastern) region is a restricted travel area due to cattle rustling and the potential concomitant violence toward any outsiders.

Kampala can also be an epicenter for political uprisings, as was the case in September of 2009 when riots began after President Museveni restricted the Buganda Kabaka's (traditional king) travel to an area which was supposedly under his rule. Buganda angry with the president's assertion of authority over their king began rioting in Kampala and the center of other towns. Tires were set ablaze in the streets, property was destroyed, and many people were injured or killed as police shifted from firing warning shots into the air to shooting into crowds to disperse mobs. Violence may erupt quickly and with little warning, so Kampala should be avoided during known political exercises that could cause conflict.

Another recent development is the presence of Somali terrorist cells within Uganda. Al Shabab took credit for the twin bombings of World Cup spectators near Kampala in July of 2010, which killed approximately 80 people, including an American missionary. While terrorism remains a threat in Uganda, there have been no incidents of violence since then. You will receive clear information about how the Peace Corps is addressing the issues of safety and security and how you can participate.

While whistles and exclamations may be fairly common on the street, this behavior can be reduced if you dress conservatively, abide by local cultural norms, and respond according to the training you will receive.

Staying Safe: Don't Be a Target for Crime

You must be prepared to take on a large degree of responsibility for your own safety. You can make yourself less of a target, ensure that your home is secure, and develop relationships in your community that will make you an unlikely victim of crime. While the factors that contribute to your risk in Uganda may be different, in many ways you can do what you would do if you moved to a new city anywhere: Be cautious, check things out, ask questions, learn about your neighborhood, know where the more risky locations are, use common sense, and be aware. You can reduce your vulnerability to crime by integrating into your community, learning the local language, acting responsibly, and abiding by Peace Corps policies and procedures. Serving safely and effectively in Uganda will require that you accept some restrictions on your current lifestyle.

Support from Staff

If a trainee or Volunteer is the victim of a safety incident, Peace Corps staff is prepared to provide support. All Peace Corps posts have procedures in place to respond to incidents of crime committed against Volunteers. The first priority for all posts in the aftermath of an incident is to ensure the Volunteer is safe and receiving medical treatment as needed. After assuring the safety of the Volunteer, Peace Corps staff response may include reassessing the Volunteer's worksite and housing arrangements and making any adjustments, as needed. In some cases, the nature of the incident may necessitate a site or housing transfer. Peace Corps staff will also assist Volunteers with preserving their rights to pursue legal sanctions against the perpetrators of the crime. It is very important that Volunteers report incidents as they occur, not only to protect their peer Volunteers, but also to preserve the future right to prosecute. Should Volunteers decide later in the process that they want to proceed with the prosecution of their assailant, this option may no longer exist if the evidence of the event has not been preserved at the time of the incident.

Crime Data for Uganda

Crime data and statistics for Uganda, which are updated yearly, are available at the following link: **http://www.peacecorps.gov/countrydata/uganda**. Please take the time to review this important information.

Few Peace Corps Volunteers are victims of serious crimes and crimes that do occur overseas are investigated and prosecuted by local authorities through the local courts system. If you are the victim of a crime, you will decide if you wish to pursue prosecution. If you decide to prosecute, Peace Corps will be there to assist you. One of our tasks is to ensure you are fully informed of your options and understand how the local legal process works. Peace Corps will help you ensure your rights are protected to the fullest extent possible under the laws of the country.

If you are the victim of a serious crime, you will learn how to get to a safe location as quickly as possible and contact your Peace Corps office. It's important that you notify Peace Corps as soon as you can so Peace Corps can provide you with the help you need.

Volunteer Safety Support in Uganda

The Peace Corps' approach to safety is a five-pronged plan to help you stay safe during your service and includes the following: information sharing, Volunteer training, site selection criteria, a detailed emergency action plan, and protocols for addressing safety and security incidents. Uganda's in-country safety program is outlined below.

The Peace Corps/Uganda office will keep you informed of any issues that may impact Volunteer safety through **information sharing**. Regular updates will be provided in Volunteer newsletters and in memorandums from the country director. In the event of a critical situation or emergency, you will be contacted through the emergency communication network. An important component of the capacity of Peace Corps to keep you informed is your buy-in to the partnership concept with the Peace Corps staff. It is expected that you will do your part in ensuring that Peace Corps staff members are kept apprised of your movements in-country so they are able to inform you.

Volunteer training will include sessions on specific safety and security issues in Uganda. This training will prepare you to adopt a culturally appropriate lifestyle and exercise judgment that promotes safety and reduces risk in your home, at work, and while traveling. Safety training is offered throughout service and is integrated into the language, cross-cultural aspects, health, and other components of training. You will be expected to successfully complete all training competencies in a variety of areas, including safety and security, as a condition of service.

Certain **site selection criteria** are used to determine safe housing for Volunteers before their arrival. The Peace Corps staff works closely with host communities and counterpart agencies to help prepare them for a Volunteer's arrival and to establish expectations of their respective roles in supporting the Volunteer. Each site is inspected before the Volunteer's arrival to ensure placement in appropriate, safe, and secure housing and worksites. Site selection is based, in part, on any relevant site history; access to medical, banking, postal, and other essential services; availability of communications, transportation, and markets; different housing options and living arrangements; and other Volunteer support needs.

You will also learn about Peace Corps/Uganda's **detailed emergency action plan**, which is implemented in the event of civil or political unrest or a natural disaster. When you arrive at your site, you will complete and submit a site locator form with your address, contact information, and a map to your house. If there is a security threat, you will gather with other Volunteers in Uganda at predetermined locations until the situation is resolved or the Peace Corps decides to evacuate.

Finally, in order for the Peace Corps to be fully responsive to the needs of Volunteers, it is imperative that Volunteers immediately report any security incident to the Peace Corps office. The Peace Corps has established protocols for **addressing safety and security incidents** in a timely and appropriate manner, and it collects and evaluates safety and security data to track trends and develop strategies to minimize risks to future Volunteers.

DIVERSITY AND CROSS-CULTURAL ISSUES

In fulfilling its mandate to share the face of America with host countries, the Peace Corps is making special efforts to assure that all of America's richness is reflected in the Volunteer corps. More Americans of color are serving in today's Peace Corps than at any time in recent history. Differences in race, ethnic background, age, religion, and sexual orientation are expected and welcomed among our Volunteers. Part of the Peace Corps' mission is to help dispel any notion that Americans are all of one origin or race and to establish that each of us is as thoroughly American as the other despite our many differences.

Our diversity helps us accomplish that goal. In other ways, however, it poses challenges. In Uganda, as in other Peace Corps host countries, Volunteers' behavior, lifestyle, background, and beliefs are judged in a cultural context very different from their own. Certain personal perspectives or characteristics commonly accepted in the United States may be quite uncommon, unacceptable, or even repressed in Uganda.

Outside of Uganda's capital, residents of rural communities have had relatively little direct exposure to other cultures, races, religions, and lifestyles. What people view as typical American behavior or norms may be a misconception, such as the belief that all Americans are rich and have blond hair and blue eyes. The people of Uganda are justly known for their generous hospitality to foreigners; however, members of the community in which you will live may display a range of reactions to cultural differences that you present.

To ease the transition and adapt to life in Uganda, you may need to make some temporary, yet fundamental compromises in how you present yourself as an American and as an individual. For example, female trainees and Volunteers may not be able to exercise the independence available to them in the United States; political discussions need to be handled with great care; and some of your personal beliefs may best remain undisclosed. You will need to develop techniques and personal strategies for coping with these and other limitations. The Peace Corps staff will lead diversity and sensitivity discussions during pre-service training and will be on call to provide support, but the challenge ultimately will be your own.

Overview of Diversity in Uganda

The Peace Corps staff in Uganda recognizes the adjustment issues that come with diversity and will endeavor to provide support and guidance. During pre-service training, several sessions will be held to discuss diversity and coping mechanisms. We look forward to having male and female Volunteers from a variety of races, ethnic groups, ages, religions, and sexual orientations, and hope that you will become part of a diverse group of Americans who take pride in supporting one another and demonstrating the richness of American culture.

What Might a Volunteer Face?

Possible Issues for Female Volunteers

Equality of the sexes is generally considered irrelevant in Ugandan culture, as distinct roles and responsibilities are expected of men and women. Female Volunteers often encounter extremely conservative attitudes regarding gender equality. Likewise, the behavior of female Volunteers is more often scrutinized and criticized than that of their male peers. Although the Peace Corps emphasizes sensitivity toward other cultures, it may occasionally be necessary to explain why you believe something or behave a certain way— but only you can determine when and if such an explanation is worthwhile. Neither men nor women are considered adults until they are married and have children. This being the case, female Volunteers should expect curiosity from Ugandan friends regarding their marital status and whether they have children.

Possible Issues for Volunteers of Color

Skin color and appearance, more than actual heritage, often influence how Volunteers are perceived and treated by their host communities. Even if they can convince Ugandans that they are indeed American, Volunteers who do not fit the mold of the "typical" American may still not be regarded as "true" Americans. African-American Volunteers often express frustration or disappointment at being asked, "What are you?" and having Ugandans show genuine shock or amazement when they answer "African American" or "black American." Ugandans often react with disbelief and ask, "But where are your parents from?"

African-American women should be aware that they may be perceived as Ugandan women and, thus, be treated as such. This can be an asset in some situations and a challenge in others. African-American women may find that their behavior is scrutinized more closely than that of white women.

Asian-American Volunteers express frustration at being assumed to be Chinese or Japanese, rather than American. Because of the kung fu movies shown throughout the country, some Asian Americans have been asked if they know kung fu. This may seem humorous at first, but can eventually become tiresome. Americans of South Asian descent, whether Indian, Sri Lankan, Bangladeshi, or Pakistani, are collectively referred to as Indians or Asians, rather than Americans. Some Ugandans may feel resentment toward people with a South Asian background because of the unequal treatment received by Ugandans and South Asian residents of Uganda during the period of British colonialism. On the flip side, Volunteers of color may also be surprised to find that Ugandans consider them to be American or European, regardless of their color, and refer to them using words normally used to describe white people.

Possible Issues for Senior Volunteers

Age can also determine how a Volunteer is perceived and treated by Ugandans. Older Volunteers may be respected for their wisdom, but may face challenges in being fully accepted in the workplace. Ugandans can be especially curious about older female Volunteers and puzzled as to why they have no spouse or children, even if they have the pictures to prove otherwise. In addition, since most Volunteers are younger than 30, it may be difficult for older Volunteers to develop friendships and gain the necessary support among the most accessible group—other Peace Corps Volunteers.

Possible Issues for Gay, Lesbian, or Bisexual Volunteers

Gay and lesbian Volunteers need to know that Uganda has a very conservative society. Homosexuality is illegal (with a possible sentence of 17 years to life imprisonment), and many Ugandans deny that homosexuality actually exists in their culture. Any display of your sexual orientation will, at best, be severely frowned upon and, at worst, may threaten your safety and security. Most previous gay, lesbian, or bisexual Volunteers in Uganda have decided to not be open about their sexual orientation. Prior to accepting an assignment in Uganda, you should discuss this issue thoroughly with a member of the recruitment staff with whom you feel comfortable. Anyone who wants to discuss this subject further once in Uganda can do so in confidence with a Peace Corps staff member.

A recommended resource for support and advice prior to and during your service is the Lesbian, Gay, Bisexual & Transgender U.S. Peace Corps Alumni website at **www.lgbrpcv.org**.

Possible Religious Issues for Volunteers

Whether you practice a religion or not, you will probably find Ugandan approaches to spirituality different from what you are used to. You will certainly gain a deeper understanding over your two years of service, but initially, the most disconcerting thing may be the constant open discussion of religion. You should be prepared to be asked if you are a Christian, if you are "saved," and if there are any Muslims in America. You may be stared at in disbelief if you state you do not believe in God. Your tolerance of, and willingness to answer, such questions will serve you well.

Possible Issues for Volunteers With Disabilities

As part of the medical clearance process, the Peace Corps Office of Medical Services determined that you were physically and emotionally capable, with or without reasonable accommodations, to perform a full tour of Volunteer service in Uganda without unreasonable risk of harm to yourself or interruption of service. The Peace Corps/ Uganda staff will work with disabled Volunteers to make reasonable accommodations for them in training, housing, jobsites, or other areas to enable them to serve safely and effectively.

Ugandans with disabilities are generally treated no differently than other Ugandans (hence the lack of special schools or accommodations for those with disabilities) and are expected to complete the same work, though not necessarily using the same methods.

While this section on diversity may be unsettling to some of you, we want you to be prepared for the many challenges you are about to face. Know that "non-stereotypical" Volunteers have had excellent experiences in Uganda. Ultimately, only you can shape your time in Uganda as a Volunteer, but Peace Corps/Uganda is here to support you along the way.

FREQUENTLY ASKED QUESTIONS

This list has been compiled by Volunteers serving in Uganda and is based on their experience. Use it as an informal guide in making your own list, bearing in mind that each experience is individual. There is no perfect list! You obviously cannot bring everything on the list, so consider those items that make the most sense to you personally and professionally. You can always have things sent to you later. As you decide what to bring, keep in mind that you have a 100-pound weight limit on baggage. And remember, you can get almost everything you need in Uganda.

How much luggage am I allowed to bring to Uganda?

Most airlines have baggage size and weight limits and assess charges for transport of baggage that exceeds those limits. The Peace Corps has its own size and weight limits and will not pay the cost of transport for baggage that exceeds these limits. The Peace Corps' allowance is two checked pieces of luggage with combined dimensions of both pieces not to exceed 107 inches (length + width + height) and a carry-on bag with dimensions of no more than 45 inches. Checked baggage should not exceed 100 pounds total with a maximum weight of 50 pounds for any one bag.

Peace Corps Volunteers are not allowed to take pets, weapons, explosives, radio transmitters (shortwave radios are permitted), automobiles, or motorcycles to their overseas assignments. Do not pack flammable materials or liquids such as lighter fluid, cleaning solvents, hair spray, or aerosol containers. This is an important safety precaution.

What is the electric current in Uganda?

The electric current in Uganda is 220 volts. There are surges and cuts, which can put a strain on voltage converters and appliances. The Peace Corps does not provide transformers.

How much money should I bring?

Volunteers are expected to live at the same level as the people in their community. You will be given a settling-in allowance and a monthly living allowance, which should cover your expenses. Volunteers often wish to bring additional money for vacation travel to other countries. Credit cards and traveler's checks are preferable to cash. If you choose to bring extra money, bring the amount that will suit your own travel plans and needs.

When can I take vacation and have people visit me?

Each Volunteer accrues two vacation days per month of service (excluding training). Leave may not be taken during training, the first three months of service, or the last three months of service, except in conjunction with an authorized emergency leave. Family and friends are welcome to visit you after pre-service training and the first three months of service as long as their stay does not interfere with your work. Extended stays at your site are not encouraged and may require permission from your country director. The Peace Corps is not able to provide your visitors with visa, medical, or travel assistance.

Will my belongings be covered by insurance?

The Peace Corps does not provide insurance coverage for personal effects; Volunteers are ultimately responsible for the safekeeping of their personal belongings. However, you can purchase personal property insurance before you leave. If you wish, you may contact your own insurance company; additionally, insurance application forms will be provided, and we encourage you to consider them carefully. Volunteers should not ship or take valuable items overseas. Jewelry, watches, radios, cameras, and expensive appliances are subject to loss, theft, and breakage, and in many places, satisfactory maintenance and repair services are not available.

Do I need an international driver's license?

Volunteers in Uganda do not need an international driver's license because they are prohibited from operating privately owned motorized vehicles. Most urban travel is by bus or taxi. Rural travel ranges from buses and minibuses to trucks, bicycles, and lots of walking. On very rare occasions, a Volunteer may be asked to drive a sponsor's vehicle, but this can occur only with prior written permission from the country director. Should this occur, the Volunteer may obtain a local driver's license. A U.S. driver's license will facilitate the process, so bring it with you just in case.

What should I bring as gifts for Uganda friends and my host family?

This is not a requirement. A token of friendship is sufficient. Some gift suggestions include knickknacks for the house; pictures, books, or calendars of American scenes; souvenirs from your area; hard candies that will not melt or spoil; or photos to give away.

Where will my site assignment be when I finish training and how isolated will I be?

Peace Corps trainees are not assigned to individual sites until after they have completed pre-service training. This gives Peace Corps staff the opportunity to assess each trainee's technical and language skills prior to assigning sites, in addition to finalizing site selections with their ministry counterparts. If feasible, you may have the opportunity to provide input on your site preferences, including geographical location, distance from other Volunteers, and living conditions. However, keep in mind that many factors influence the site selection process and that the Peace Corps cannot guarantee placement where you would ideally like to be. Most Volunteers live in small towns or in rural villages and are usually within one hour from another Volunteer. Some sites require a 10- to 12-hour drive from the capital.

How can my family contact me in an emergency?

The Peace Corps' Office of Special Services (OSS) provides assistance in handling emergencies affecting trainees and Volunteers or their families. Before leaving the United States, instruct your family to notify the Office of Special Services immediately if an emergency arises, such as a serious illness or death of a family member. During normal business hours, the number for the Office of Special Services is 855.855.1961, then select option 2; or directly at 202-692-1470. After normal business hours and on weekends and holidays, the OSS duty officer can be reached at the above number. For non-emergency questions, your family can get information from your country desk staff at the Peace Corps by calling 855.855.1961.

Can I call home from Uganda?

Yes, if there is good cellular phone network coverage. Calls from Uganda to the United States are very expensive. We recommend Skype, letter writing, and setting up periodic calls from home. Prepaid phone cards from the United States do not work in Uganda.

Should I bring a cellular phone with me?

The systems in Uganda are different from those typically used in the United States. The good news is that the costs of service are going down and the coverage is almost everywhere. Most Volunteers have chosen to purchase cell phones in Uganda during pre-service training. A phone from America has to be an unlocked phone and Volunteers should check the specifics of any phone for international capabilities.

Will there be email and Internet access? Should I bring my computer?

There are places throughout Uganda that provide Internet services; although proximity to those services will vary depending on site placement. The Peace Corps office in Kampala has computers with Internet that are for Volunteer/trainee use only. Although there is no guarantee that you will be placed at a site that has electricity, Volunteers in Uganda who brought their laptops are generally glad they did. They can be useful for work purposes or to type emails before going into town to use the Internet, saving time to catch up on old emails. Some Volunteers are also connected to Skype, allowing them to keep in better contact with family and friends. It is recommended that you purchase personal property insurance to cover costs for all electronic equipment in case they are damaged or stolen. Peace Corps partners with Clements International and information on personal property insurance through them is in your invitation packet.

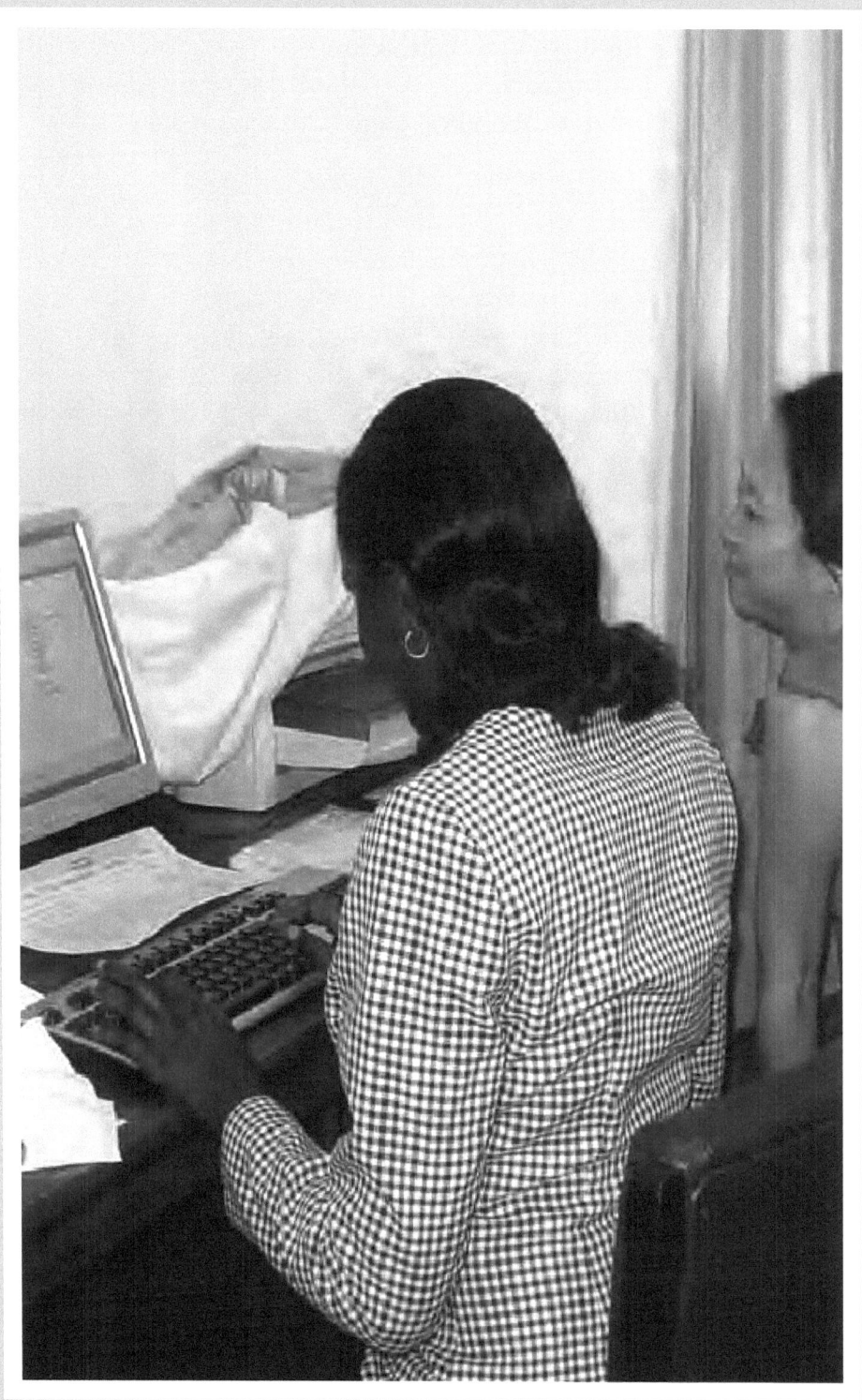

WELCOME LETTERS FROM COUNTRY VOLUNTEERS

I live at a primary school with more than 900 primary school girls; one might think that might get to be a bit much, and honestly, there have been days where I've felt overwhelmed, but I couldn't have asked for a better placement. The people here are so gracious, so welcoming, and so friendly.

I'll never forget the first day at my site. We were still in training, but we were visiting our sites to get an idea of what it was going to be like out on our own. I arrived at the school and before the gate there were hundreds of girls. They had all heard I was coming that afternoon and were very excited. They greeted me in the local language and argued about who would help me with my bags. Sister Kevin, the headmistress at the school, gave me a tour of my house. I could tell they had worked very hard to get the place ready for me. The house was in great shape and someone had painted "You are most welcome, Christine" on the wall. I overlooked the fact that they had misspelled my name, especially since the three or four days I was there they treated me so wonderfully. They brought me all my meals and helped me get acquainted with the school compound and the town.

Since then, and I've been here for a year now, the hospitality really hasn't changed all that much. There aren't more than 100 girls rushing to me, fighting over who will help with my bags anymore — thank goodness — but it's still amazing how good they are to me. I have tried several times to fetch my own water, but I can rarely walk 10 steps out my door without somebody insisting on helping me. I have a group of kids who come over nearly every evening to visit or sometimes to help me with laundry or dishes if I need it. I never ask the kids; they just jump right in. I enjoy their company most of the time; they remind me, on rough days, why I am here.

I can't stress enough how amazing the people here are. I think a lot about the projects that I've been working on and what I am contributing, but I know the people of Budaka, Uganda, have taught me a whole lot more than I could ever teach them.

Dear New Volunteer,

Welcome to the Peace Corps family, and welcome to Uganda, your home away from home for the next two years. Uganda, as Winston Churchill said, is the Pearl of Africa. Its border stretches along the shores of Lake Victoria to the south, the Great Rift Valley to the east, the beautiful Mountains of the Moon to the west, and the flowing savannahs of the northern plains, enclosing one of the most diverse landscapes on the continent. And because Uganda is situated on the equator, the weather is always gorgeous!

Along with this diverse landscape, you will find a plethora of cultures, with rich heritages that have spanned centuries. There are 48 different tribes in Uganda, each with its own language and customs. The southern part of the country is mainly composed of Bantu-speaking tribes, while the north consists of Nilolitic speakers. Each of these tribes has shaped Uganda as a country, and this diversity has been critical in fostering the dialogue that made Uganda a leader in the fight against HIV/AIDS.

As a Volunteer, you will have the opportunity to live and work with some of the nicest people in the world. The rewards from such an experience are immeasurable. This does not mean your task will not be free of challenges. There are countless villages in Uganda that lack power, running water, and the other amenities you are accustomed to having at home. Along with this, you are being asked to live and work in a completely new environment with its own social norms and customs. Your decision might begin to seem overwhelming, and this is understandable because you are about to embark on a life-changing journey. But you are not going on it alone.

You will have access to the best staff in the world! The staff at Peace Corps/Uganda is dedicated to making your stay in Uganda as comfortable as possible. Plus, you will have your fellow Volunteers who will be there for you.

Once again, welcome to Peace Corps and welcome to Uganda.

Dear Future Volunteer,

The feelings you must be experiencing right now with your Peace Corps invitation in hand and an impending departure date seem like only yesterday for me. I remember well the long, long to-do list, packets of even more paperwork, packing and re-packing, anxious thoughts, and teary goodbyes. There were certainly moments when I wondered if it would ever really happen. I am happy to report that everything will indeed work out; you will finally set foot in-country, and Peace Corps/Uganda is worth every sleepless night!

Pre-service training provides a smooth adjustment into a new country and a new culture. Peace Corps staff members form a dedicated team. They help you land as gracefully as possible. Homestay families warmly welcome new Volunteers, do their best to make you comfortable, and often make you feel as if you're a member of the family. The training schedule will keep you busy and you will surely wonder where 10 weeks went when the day comes to finally move to your site—your new home for the next two years. It is then that this experience begins to feel less like a whirlwind, and more like a new reality.

The challenges in the beginning soon become nothing. You discover where to buy the best tomatoes, the most efficient way to collect your water, and how to catch a ride to the nearest town. Adjusting to no electricity, cooking over charcoal, bathing with a bucket, and using a pit latrine quickly begin to feel perfectly normal. (OK, let's just say normal.)

Eventually, it becomes easier and easier to venture further into your village, test fledgling language skills, and generate ideas about what exactly you will be doing for the next 24 months. Relationships begin to form, and then, there's finally the day when you refer to your site as "home" without even thinking about it; when your neighbor asks if "you've been lost" and offers you a sweet, juicy pineapple upon your return; when a child greets you with a smile of recognition at the borehole; when a colleague invites you to her daughter's introduction; or when a muzee (elder) shows you a better way to light your charcoal. You will feel an invaluable sense of warmth and acceptance. You will recognize these as small steps when there are the inevitable moments of frustration or lingering questions about whether or not you are really making any progress.

In the beginning, 24 months seems like such a long time to be away from America. Already, I recognize that it is such a short time to be here in Uganda. Yes, there was a day when 12 hours of sunlight felt like three times as much as I knew what to do with, but I know in the end, I'll look back and wish I spent every second absorbing it all. I'm doing my best to do just that because now I can see it will all go by in a flash. Each day of this experience opens minds and possibilities and that, to me, is one of the greatest things you have to look forward to in Peace Corps/Uganda.

Best wishes with the rest of your to-do list, see you soon, and safe journey!

PACKING LIST

This list has been compiled by Volunteers serving in Uganda and is based on their experience. Use it as an informal guide in making your own list, bearing in mind that each experience is individual. There is no perfect list! You obviously cannot bring everything on the list, so consider those items that make the most sense to you personally and professionally. You can always have things sent to you later. As you decide what to bring, keep in mind that you have an 100-pound weight limit on baggage. And remember, you can get almost everything you need in Uganda.

Take a deep breath. Everything you NEED, you can find in-country. Quality, selection, or prices may not be exactly what you want, so if you're particular about a certain product (such as the exclusive use of Pantene Extra Body conditioner), bring enough for three or four months. It usually takes 6-8 weeks for those special packages to arrive, but can take longer. If you aren't picky or don't want to buy the nonessentials, that's cool too! The used markets and local tailors are great here, but you won't be able to shop much while in training and it doesn't hurt to be prepared, so check out the list below. Your interests and lifestyle choices probably won't change that much, so only bring hiking boots if you like to hike or an appointment book if you like to pencil things in. Buy fewer items at outdoor stores than you think you should have, and instead bring the comfort items that make you feel good. Remember, you could always have your friends or family send you things you really miss so try not to over-do it.

General Clothing

For men:

- 2 pairs of slacks
- 3-4 collared shirts
- Belt
- 1 tie

For women:

- 2-3 skirts below the knee, not see through/with a slip
- 4-8 shirts (dressy/business casual, not spaghetti straps!)
- 2 casual T-shirts for hanging out
- Good bras/sports bras (good support is not available here!); remember, you will have to cover up too
- Culottes. Shorts/leggings to go under skirt for bike riding
- Nice clothes you would wear out with your friends in the U.S.

For all:

- Something casual you enjoy wearing; jeans, gauchos, etc.
- 1 sweater, light jacket, fleece, sweatshirt, or long sleeve shirt
- Nice clothes you would wear out with your friends in the U.S.
- Exercise clothes
- Good underwear (local selection is not of good quality)
- Raincoat/poncho
- 1 dressy outfit for official functions (tie for men sports jacket optional; dress for women)
- PJs
- Bathing suit

Shoes

- Nice comfortable shoes (think nice sandals, Tevas and Chacos give adiscount to PCVs)
- Comfortable flat dress shoes for work and official events; dressy sandals are acceptable and a lot more comfortable
- Running shoes (if you run)

Personal Hygiene and Toiletry Items

- Toiletries to last a month
- Tampons/Diva Cup (pads and OB are widely available)

Miscellaneous

- 2 pairs of glasses/sunglasses
- Three-month supply of prescription medication
- Favorite one-month supply of sunscreen and insect repellent
- Towel (camping/travel ones are nice because they're compact, dry quickly and are easy to wash); you can buy decent towels in country.
- Headlamp with spare bulb; or flashlight
- 2 flat bed sheets for homestay (you don't know what size bed you'll have)
- Medium book/messenger bag (for 3-4 day trips)
- Batteries (If you bring things that take them; rechargable are a great idea)
- Power Adapter (If you bring electronics)

Not necessary but useful for some volunteers

- 1 reusable water bottle
- Camera (advise not to bring large camera bags)
- Shortwave/FM radio (available here)
- Favorite recipes
- Duct tape
- Watch
- Portable alarm clock
- Peace Corps provides decent pillows and blankets at the beginning of training
- Good quality rope
- Games/cards
- Bandana/hat
- Plastic mattress cover
- Tennis shoes/hiking boots
- Leatherman/Swiss Army knife
- Laptop computer (see Technology section in Welcome Book)
- Music in whatever form you enjoy (iPod, other MP3, CD player + CDs, tapes)
- Good pens (if it's important to you, BIC pens are available)
- Seeds (spices, veggies, etc.—can be purchased here or mailed later)
- Beauty products/pampering items (nail polish, eyeliner) for de-stressing (if you use them)
- Money (not necessary, but you may want to have. $50 or $100 bills dated after 2003 will get the best exchange rate. No more than $300 is recommended in cash.)
- Debit/credit card (again not necessary, but if you do bring one, Visa is MUCH better than others)
- 1 nice kitchen knife; can opener (if you cook or have interest) a decent chef or Santoku is a great item to have
- Vegetable peeler (so many useful meals)

Even less essential but nice for some

- Regional spice blend (Lawry's, Old Bay, Cavender's, Mrs. Dash, Asian spices, seaweed, etc.); taco seasoning

- Tea tree oil (great antiseptic for skin infections and mosquito bites)
- Razors (available but very expensive)
- Small ball; bike pump
- Good compact umbrella (available)
- Ziploc bags/Tupperwave
- English dictionary (available)
- Money belt
- Spare flashlight (available)
- Smartphone for Internet (Nokia E71/E72 recommended)
- Light sleeping bag and ground pad
- Light tent
- Small toolkit or bicycle repair kit
- Solar charger for batteries/electronics (available)

Gift Ideas for Host Families (You can buy something here also)

- Regional calendar/souvenirs from your home area
- Dollar store items (tacky is in the eye of the beholder)
- Coloring books, markers, stickers
- Pocket knives, nice flashlights
- Candy, food items
- Perfume made in the U.S.

We recommend you spend time with family first and get to know what they may truly enjoy in their lives, then buy it in Uganda (trays, cups, games, etc.).

Don't Bring

- Too many books (PCVs are good at sharing)
- Short skirts (at or above the knee)
- Too many pairs of shorts (not common for adults to wear)
- Too many white clothes (they turn brown quickly)
- Tight clothes (culturally inappropriate)
- Too many socks (available here)
- Over-the-counter medication, insect repellent, sunscreen, or multivitamins (PC provides these)

Other notes

- Lock your luggage, preferably using TSA-approved locks. This is useful in transit, at homestay, and while traveling during your service.

- Volunteers are encouraged to consider personal property insurance to cover the maintenance and replacement of computer equipment that they may bring overseas or purchase in-country.

At your departure airport in the U.S., security will often screen your luggage upon entering the terminal. It is advisable to pack all sharp objects near the top of one of your bags. In the event that they do search your bag, they will hold onto these items until you check your bags at the ticket counter.

PRE-DEPARTURE CHECKLIST

The following list consists of suggestions for you to consider as you prepare to live outside the United States for two years. Not all items will be relevant to everyone, and the list does not include everything you should make arrangements for.

Family

- Notify family that they can call the Peace Corps' Counseling and Outreach Unit at any time if there is a critical illness or death of a family member (24-hour telephone number: 1-855-855-1961, then press 2; or directly at 202-692-1470).

- Give the Peace Corps' On the Home Front handbook to family and friends.

Passport/Travel

- Forward to the Peace Corps travel office all paperwork for the Peace Corps passport and visas.

- Verify that your luggage meets the size and weight limits for international travel.

- Obtain a personal passport if you plan to travel after your service ends. (Your Peace Corps passport will expire three months after you finish your service, so if you plan to travel longer, you will need a regular passport.)

Medical/Health

- Complete any needed dental and medical work.

- If you wear glasses, bring two pairs.

- Arrange to bring a three-month supply of all medications (including birth control pills) you are currently taking.

Insurance

- Make arrangements to maintain life insurance coverage.

- Arrange to maintain supplemental health coverage while you are away. (Even though the Peace Corps is responsible for your health care during Peace Corps service overseas, it is advisable for people who have pre-existing conditions to arrange for the continuation of their supplemental health coverage. If there is a lapse in coverage, it is often difficult and expensive to be reinstated.)

- Arrange to continue Medicare coverage if applicable.

Personal Papers

- Bring a copy of your certificate of marriage or divorce.

Voting

- Register to vote in the state of your home of record. (Many state universities consider voting and payment of state taxes as evidence of residence in that state.)

- Obtain a voter registration card and take it with you overseas.

- Arrange to have an absentee ballot forwarded to you overseas.

Personal Effects

- Purchase personal property insurance to extend from the time you leave your home for service overseas until the time you complete your service and return to the United States.

Financial Management

- Keep a bank account in your name in the U.S.

- Obtain student loan deferment forms from the lender or loan service.

- Execute a Power of Attorney for the management of your property and business.

- Arrange for deductions from your readjustment allowance to pay alimony, child support, and other debts through the Office of Volunteer Financial Operations at 855.855.1961, extension 1770.

- Place all important papers—mortgages, deeds, stocks, and bonds—in a safe deposit box or with an attorney or other caretaker.

CONTACTING PEACE CORPS HEADQUARTERS

This list of numbers will help connect you with the appropriate office at Peace Corps headquarters to answer various questions. You can use the toll-free number and extension or dial directly using the local numbers provided. Be sure to leave the toll-free number and extensions with your family so they can contact you in the event of an emergency.

Peace Corps Headquarters Toll-free Number: 855.855.1961, Press 1 or ext. # (see below)

Peace Corps' Mailing Address:

Peace Corps Headquarters
1111 20th Street, NW
Washington, DC 20526

Questions About:	Staff:	Toll-Free Ext:	Direct/Local #:
Responding to an Invitation	Office of Placement	x1840	202.692.1840
Country Information	Melaney Monreal Starling Desk Officer / (Uganda, Burkina Faso, Mali & Niger) Uganda@peacecorps.gov	X2612	202.692.2612
Plane Tickets, Passports, Visas, or other travel matters:	CWT SATO Travel	x1170	202.692.1170
Legal Clearance	Office of Placement	x1840	202.692.1840
Medical Clearance & Forms Processing (includes dental)	Screening Nurse	x1500	202.692.1500
Medical Reimbursements (handled by a subcontractor)	Seven Corners	N/A	202.692.1538 800.335.0611
Loan Deferments, Taxes, Financial Operations	Office Of Volunteer and PSC Financial Services	x1770	202.692.1770
Readjustment Allowance Withdrawals, Power of Attorney, Staging (Pre-Departure Orientation), and Reporting Instructions	Office of Staging *Note: You will receive comprehensive information (hotel and flight arrangements) three to five weeks prior to departure. This information is not available sooner.*	x1865	202.692.1865
Family Emergencies (to get information to a Volunteer overseas) 24 hours	Office of Special Services	x1470	202.692.1470